Bertha Meriton Cordery Gardiner

A Secret Negociation with Charles the First, 1643-1644

Bertha Meriton Cordery Gardiner

A Secret Negociation with Charles the First, 1643-1644

ISBN/EAN: 9783337015954

Printed in Europe, USA, Canada, Australia, Japan

Cover: Foto ©Suzi / pixelio.de

More available books at **www.hansebooks.com**

THE CAMDEN MISCELLANY,

VOLUME THE EIGHTH:

CONTAINING

PRINTED FOR THE CAMDEN SOCIETY.

M.DCCC.LXXXIII.

A SECRET NEGOCIATION

WITH

CHARLES THE FIRST.

1643—1644.

EDITED,

FROM THE TANNER MSS. IN THE BODLEIAN LIBRARY,

BY

BERTHA MERITON GARDINER.

PRINTED FOR THE CAMDEN SOCIETY.

M.DCCC.LXXXIII.

PREFACE.

The following documents, from the Tanner Collection of MSS. in the Bodleian Library, are especially interesting ; in the first place, because so far as we know they contain the first overtures ever made to Charles in which the practice of religious toleration was proposed as means of effecting a settlement able to satisfy the bulk of the nation; in the second, because they help to explain how it was that the Independents, who at the beginning of the Civil war were few in number and unpopular, had become in 1645 a numerous and powerful party. Their proposal for the re-establishment of Episcopacy with a new set of bishops and toleration for those who wished to remain outside the Established Church, had the support of large numbers of persons, who had been converted into enemies of bishops by ceremonial innovations and the system of Church government upheld by Laud, but who had no theoretic or theological objections either to the service of the English Church or to Episcopacy, and to whom the idea of sub-mission to the galling yoke of the Presbyterian Church was as distasteful as to the Independents themselves.

The outline of the story of the negociation is as follows:—A certain Captain or, as he is sometimes called in these papers, Major Thomas Ogle, a prisoner in Winchester House, conceived the idea that those whom he terms " moderate zealous Protestants" and Independents might be induced to combine together and defend the royal cause, in order to prevent the establishment of a Presbyterian Church in

England, which appeared to be imminent, in consequence of the recent acceptance of the Solemn League and Covenant. He wrote a letter (No. 1) to the Earl of Bristol, who had at that time great influence with Charles, urging his views at length, and at the same time inclosed a paper containing six propositions (No. 2), representing the terms on which both Independents and moderate Protestants would be ready to support the King. Ogle wrote this letter on Oct. 17, 1643, but it did not leave London till the 24th of the following month : it was then sent to Oxford through Lieutenant-Colonel Mosely, one of the officers of the garrison of Aylesbury, and delivered into Bristol's hands on Dec. 2. Ogle says in this letter that as proof of good faith Aylesbury should be delivered up to the King's forces ; and it seems probable that it was through him that Mosely was engaged to enter into the transaction. Ogle also informed Bristol that if the King would send a warrant ordering the keeper of Winchester House prison, Thomas Devenish, to set him at liberty, the order would be complied with. The exact time at which Ogle's plans were betrayed does not appear, but it is certain that Mosely and Devenish were prepared to give information before Ogle's letter to Bristol left London. Copies were made both of it and the Propositions, and were exhibited to some members of Parliament in all probability before Nov. 24. Mosely at some previous date, or when he forwarded Ogle's letter and the propositions, must have written to Bristol, for the first letter of his to Bristol which is in our possession (No. 3), dated Dec. 6, is clearly not the first communication that he had had with the Earl. Bristol had no knowledge of Ogle, but complied with his requests, forwarding a warrant to Devenish to set him at liberty, also a safe conduct with a blank left for the insertion of names, and further, a bill of exchange for 100l. to enable him to pay his expenses and make his way to Oxford. These documents were all forwarded to Mosely at Aylesbury, and taken by him to London, where they were examined by Lord Wharton, Gerard, and Clotworthy on Dec. 11. Ogle was afterwards suffered to escape [a] and go to Oxford, where he arrived on Jan. 3, and received an encouraging reception both from Bristol and the King. From Oxford, besides writing to Devenish, Ogle wrote to the Independent ministers, Goodwyn and Nye, who were members of the Assembly of Divines, then sitting in London, urging on them to come to Oxford, and informing Nye that the King was prepared to make him his chaplain.

Unfortunately the whole of the correspondence relating to this affair is not in the Tanner Collection. It appears, however, from the entries in the Journals, that Devenish wrote to Bristol offering to betray Windsor Castle, and that the Earl replied, approving of the design and sending to him a royal warrant to raise 200 men under his son's command to put into that garrison.[b] Charles also wrote a letter to Mosely, shortly before the royal forces marched against Aylesbury, in which he instructed him, in case the plan of surrender failed, to blow up the powder magazine.[c] On Sunday night, Jan. 21, in spite of a heavy fall of snow, the royalists approached the town, but only to find that they were deceived, and to withdraw again to Oxford with the loss of many lives in consequence of the inclement weather. Those who had cognizance of the negociation doubtless had allowed it to continue so long with the object of getting the better of the King, but it was not possible that Charles

---

[a] Ogle was son-in-law to Peter Smart, former prebendary of Durham Cathedral (see No. 13, note). On Dec. 28 Smart petitioned the House of Lords that his son Ogle might be at liberty to go abroad with a keeper, as in consequence of his imprisonment he cannot prosecute or prepare for the hearing of his cause.—L. J. vol. vi. p. 355. On Jan. 6 is the further entry :—" That whereas this House ordered that Captain Ogle should have liberty to go abroad with a keeper to solicit for Mr. Smart in his business, the said Ogle is ran away."—L. J. vol. vi. p. 367.

[b] C. J. vol. iii. p. 378. The King also wrote a letter to Devenish, dated Jan. 12.—L. J. vol. vi. p. 394.

[c] L. J. vol. vi. p. 394. C. J. vol. iii. p. 378.

should be longer hoodwinked, and on Jan. 26 Lord Wharton brought the affair before the notice of the House of Lords.

Like most conspirators, Ogle immensely overrated his own importance and underrated the difficulties in the way of the execution of his plans.   But it is none the less probable that the propositions which he forwarded really represented the views of those whose spokesman he declared himself to be.   He informed Bristol that they were drawn up by the advice of some of the principal men on each side, and there is no reason for doubting his word on this point.   It is evident from his letters to Goodwyn and Nye that he was personally acquainted with both of them, and it is of course possible that men too honourable and too far-sighted to enter into treasonable plots for the betrayal of garrison towns may yet have been willing in the first instance to take advantage of Ogle's overtures in order to discover whether there was hope that Charles would ever be ready to make peace on terms acceptable to them. There is besides reason for concluding that the Parliament felt more uneasiness than it cared to confess, since in opposition to the usual practice in such cases as little publicity as possible was given to the details of the negociaticn.   No advantage whatever could be gained by spreading abroad such intelligence as that the Independents and Brownists had drawn up a very high and daring petition, threatening if the Scots covenant were forced upon them to lay down their arms;[a] a fact hitherto so well concealed that no notice of it had appeared in any of the numerous papers and pamphlets published on either side.

At the same time that Charles through the Earl of Bristol was negociating with Ogle, through Lord Digby, Bristol's son, he was carrying on a second negociation with other persons in London.[b] This negociation was discovered and made public (Jan. 6) about three weeks before information concerning Ogle's plans was laid

---

[a] See p. 5.   [b] Referred to by Ogle, No. 23.

before Parliament; and the different course pursued on the
two occasions reveals how differently the Parliament felt itself
affected by the two transactions. Two Roman Catholics, Sir Basil
Brooke and Colonel Read,[a] endeavoured to prevail on various
influential men in the city to enter into a plan of engaging the
Corporation of London to present peace propositions to Charles.
The desire for peace that existed in London as well as the national
jealousy of the Scots were the levers by aid of which the contrivers
hoped to effect their design. Thomas Violet, a goldsmith, who had
been imprisoned for refusing to pay a tax imposed by the Parliament, and Theophilus Riley, the scout-master of the city, both took
part in the business, and Violet, as well as an under-agent Wood,
conveyed letters from Digby and Read[b] at Oxford to Riley and
Brooke in London. Hints of the design were made to various
persons known to be desirous of speedily bringing the war to an
end,—Alderman Gibbes, Sir David Watkins, and others. Sir David
Watkins appears at once to have given information to certain
members of the House of Commons. Both Violet and Riley, when
examined, denied that it had been their intention to engage the
city to act independently of the Parliament; but from the evidence
brought before it the Parliament was perfectly justified in concluding that the King's object was to inveigle the Corporation to

---

[a] Read, a Scotchman by birth, was a Roman Catholic, and had held the charge
of lieutenant-general in Strafford's army in Ireland. The revolted Irish had
employed him to negociate for them with the Lords Justices, but on his arrival at
Dublin he was seized and racked. He was afterwards sent to London along
with Lord Maguire and MacMahon (see No. 3, note).—*History of the Irish
Confederation and War in Ireland* 1641-1643, edited by John T. Gilbert, vol. i.
pp. 77, 78.

[b] Riley made use of his influence as scout-master of the city to obtain Read's
release, representing him to have been a Captain Read, made prisoner in England,
and getting him exchanged for a Parliamentarian prisoner at Oxford. Riley also
effected the release of Violet.—" *A Cunning Plot to Divide and Destroy the Par
liament and the City of London,*" *King's Pamphlets,* E.$\frac{y}{}$.

enter into a negociation with himself at Oxford, and to recognize the Assembly which was to meet at that town on Jan. 22 as the lawful Parliament of England. A letter, of which the first draft had been made in London by Violet, Brooke, and Riley, was written by the King, and addressed " To our trusty and well beloved our Lord Mayor* and Aldermen of our city of London, and all other our well-affected subjects of that city." This was committed to the care of Brooke, with instructions to cause its presentation or not, accordingly as he should think fit.

After a preamble the letter ran:—

Being informed that there is a desire in some principall persons of that city to present a petition to us, which may tend to the procuring a good understanding between us and that our city, whereby the peace of the whole kingdom may be procured, we have thought fit to let you know that we are ready to receive any such petition, and the persons who shall be appointed to present the same to us shall have a safe conduct. And you shall assure all our good subjects of that city whose hearts are touched with any sense of duty to us, or of love to the religion and laws established . . . . that we have neither passed any act, nor made any profession or protestation for the maintenance and defence of the true Protestant religion and the liberties of the subject, which we will not most strictly and religiously observe, and for the which we will not be alwaies ready to give them any security can be desired. And of these our gracious letters we expect a speedy answer from you. And so we bid you farewell. Given at our Court at Oxford, in the 19 year of our raign, 26 Dec. 1643.

Propositions were agreed on between Read, Riley, Violet, and Brooke, fit to serve as a basis for negociation. According to Brooke's evidence they were as follows:—

(1.) That the city might be satisfied that the King would settle the Protestant religion, for without that neither the Parliament nor city would admit any treaty.

(2.) That the debts contracted upon the public faith, on either side by King or Parliament, should be satisfied, and the most likeliest way for the doing thereof was to settle the excise for these purposes.

---

* Sir John Wollaston, Pennington's successor. Violet, when examined, said that he was directed by Read " to tell my Lord Mayor the King had directed his letter to him, Lord Mayor of London, hearing he was a moderate man in his place."— *A Cunning Plot*, &c., *King's Pamphlets*, E.♈.

(3.) That it was conceived that in respect of the King's declaration that the Parliament was no Parliament, and that therefore the King could not treat with them any more, this treaty was to be immediately between the King and the city, and the city was to be the medium between the King and Parliament.

And this examinat further saith, That the said Wood told the examinat that if any parliament men would joyne with the city in the treaty, they also might come with them to Oxford under the safe conduct granted to the city, though it were not exprest in the King's letter ; and that the said Wood received directions at Oxford for this examinat to declare soe much to whom he should think fit.

(4.) That there must be an act of oblivion for all parties and delinquents whatsoever, and a generall pardon. That no cessation should be expected during the treaty, if there had beene any. That no mention was made in all these Propositions either of Scotland or Ireland.

It is characteristic of Charles that he should have carried on negociations at the same time with Roman Catholics and with Independents for the recovery of his power. Most probably indeed when he allowed Ogle to make vague promises to the Independents of toleration and preferment it was not his object to effect a peace, but merely to prevail on the Parliamentary captains to surrender Aylesbury and Windsor. In the same way when he encouraged Read and Brooke in their designs he had probably little expectation of doing more than exciting feelings of ill will and jealousy between the Parliament and the City. His practice however of accepting overtures from whatever side they came had the great disadvantage that it destroyed belief in his sincerity. The readiness of the Independents to treat with him would not be increased by the discovery that he was equally ready to enter into negociations with Roman Catholics, and the Parliament, of course, did not fail to use the opportunity offered by the discovery of Brooke's plot of exciting popular prejudice against the King, and strengthening their own cause. After hearing the report of the committee which had conducted the investigations the Commons resolved:

That the matter of the report contains a seditious and jesuistical practice and design, under the fair and specious pretence of peace (having its rise and fountain from known Jesuits and Papists), to work divisions between the Parliament and the city of London ; to raise factions in both, and thereby to render them up to the designs of the enemy, and tending also to the breach of the public faith of this kingdom unto our brethren of Scotland, engaged by the late solemn covenant and treaty entered into by both nations, thereby not only to weaken us in our united forces against our popish and common enemy but also to embroil the two nations in unhappy differences.[a]

The Lords concurred in this vote, and a committee of both Houses was appointed to communicate the business at a common hall, which was held on the following Monday (Jan. 8). The report of this committee was subsequently published, together with the examinations and letters of the various persons concerned, and an intercepted copy of the proclamation lately issued by Charles at Oxford summoning the Parliament to meet at that town on Jan. 22, and offering a free pardon to any member of either House who should within that time return to his duty and allegiance.[b] The occasion was made one for a great manifestation of union. The Corporation invited the Parliament to dinner at Merchant Taylors' Hall. On the appointed day, Jan. 11, the Lords and Commons, the Scottish Commissioners, three ambassadors newly arrived from Holland, the members of the Assembly of Divines, the Lord Mayor and Corporation, Essex, Warwick, Manchester, Cromwell, and other officers of note in London, met together at Christchurch at nine in the morning to hear a thanksgiving sermon from the lips of Stephen Marshall.[c] The preacher prefaced his sermon by a curious address, which shows how eager the Presbyterian party was to prevent the idea getting abroad that division existed in London:—

"You are first met here," he said, "to feast your souls with the fat things of God's house, with a feast of fat things full of marrow, and wine on the lees well refined; and afterwards to feast your bodies with the fat things of the land and the sea, both

---

[a] C. J. vol. iii. p. 358, Jan. 6.
[b] " A cunning plot to divide and destroy the Parliament and the city of London, made known at a common hall," &c. London, Jan. 16, 1643.—*King's Pamphlets*, E. ⅗.
[c] *The Parliament Scout*, E. ¾⅔; *The Kingdom's Weekly Intelligencer*, E. ⅗.

plenty and dainty. But, if you please, you may first feast your eyes; doe but behold the face of this assembly; I dare say it will be one of the excellentest feasts that ever your eyes were refreshed with. You may first see the *two Houses of Parliament*, the honourable Lords and Commons . . . . preserved from so many treacherous designs, secret treasons, and open violences. . . . . Here you may also see *his Excellency*, the general of all our forces by land, and near him that most noble lord, the commander of our forces by sea; and with them abundance of noble and resolute commanders, all of them with their faces like unto lions. . . . . Here, also, you may behold the *representative body of the city of London*, the Lord Mayor, the Court of Aldermen, the Common Council, the *militia*, and in them the face and affection of this glorious city. *This city* . . . . after the expense of millions of treasure and thousands of lives, still as faithful and resolute to live and die in the cause of God as ever heretofore. Here you may likewise see a *reverend assembly* of grave and learned *divines*, who daily wait upon the Angel in the Mount to receive from him the lively oracles, and the patterns of God's house to present unto you. All these are of our *owne* nation; and with them you may see the *honourable, reverend, and learned Commissioners of the Church of Scotland*. . . . . All these you may behold in one view; and, which is more, you may behold them all of *one heart*. . . . . And, which is yet more, you may see them all met together this day *on purpose*, both to *praise God for this union*, and to rejoice in it, and to hold it out to all the world, and thereby to testify that, as one man, they will live and die together in this common cause of God, of our Lord Jesus Christ his Church, and these three kingdoms," &c.[a]

The sermon over, both entertainers and guests proceeded in procession from the church to Merchant Taylors' Hall, while on the way the London trained bands lined the streets on either side:—

The first that went forth were the Common Councilmen and militia of London in their gowns; after them the Lord Mayor and Court of Aldermen in their scarlet gowns, on horseback, with their officers and attendants; next came the Lord General and Lord Admiral together, with about sixteen earls and lords of the upper House of Parliament, and divers colonels and military commanders, all on foot; and immediately after them came near two hundred of the worthy members of the House of Commons; and then the Commissioners of Scotland; and after all these about eighty divines of the Reverend Assembly: all which did much content and delight the spectators to see these so noble, faithful, religious, and honourable pillars of the truth, and maintainers of their rights and privileges, and patrons of the true religion, appear with so united a concurrence of hearts and spirits.[b]

---

[a] "A sacred Panegyrick, or a sermon of Thanksgiving."—*King's Pamphlets*, E. 보. The italics are as in the original.

[b] *The True Informer, King's Pamphlets*, E. 44.

At Cheapside an entertainment was prepared for the spectators, specially suitable to this celebration of the discovery of a plot in which, happily for the Parliament, Roman Catholics were concerned. At Cheapside, where the cross formerly stood, light scaffoldings of firwood had been raised, "all hung round with pictures and popish trinkets, which caused a very thronged fair . . . . there was crucifixes, and cunjering boxes, and velvet crosses, and crosses embroidered with gold. There was the Virgin Mary crowned Queen of Heaven . . . there was magic spells and jacks in boxes. The bishops' crucifix, Jesus, and the nuns' holy bushes," along with candlesticks, images, beads, trinkets, and similar relics of past times. As the procession passed by these erections were set on fire, and were speedily reduced to ashes. "The smoke of the flames," says one of the papers, "like incense ascended towards heaven, as that which was acceptable to God."

While the crowd amused itself with the bonfire the members of Parliament and other guests dined in the Hall. At the close of the entertainment Dr. Burgess, one of the members of the Assembly of Divines, surprised the company by ascending the gallery, where musicians formerly sat on festive occasions, and proposing that all should join in singing the 85th Psalm. With this testimony of union and thankfulness the proceedings were brought to an end.[a] The following Sunday, Jan. 21, was kept as a day of public thanksgiving, and the vote of the two Houses passed on the discovery of the plot read in the city churches.[b]

The effusions of the weekly papers and the address which Marshall thought necessary to affix to his sermon make the reader incline to exclaim, "Methinks the gentlemen do protest too much." With regard to all that concerned Catholics and Catholicism,

---

[a] *King's Pamphlets, Mercurius*, &c. E. ᵧ; *The Scottish Dove*, E. ⁴⁴⁄₂; *The True Informer*, E. ²⁴⁄₂.

[b] C. J. vol. iii. p. 370; L. J. vol. vi. p. 384.

the Parliament, the Assembly of Divines, the City, the militia, and the army, might with justice assert that they presented an united front; but the procession in which marched side by side such men as Cromwell and Manchester contained elements which before the year had passed would be unable longer to work together. As yet, however, only the beginnings of division had appeared; and although evidences of ill-feeling between Presbyterians and Independents were not wanting, these took rather a personal than a political form, the Independents remaining stedfastly loyal to the side of the Parliament, expecting when the King was beaten that some solution of the religious question would be arrived at satisfactory to themselves. It is remarkable that, while Ogle was seeking to win Goodwyn and Nye to desert the side of the Parliament, overtures of like character were being made through another source to the younger Sir Henry Vane. Lord Lovelace wrote a letter to Vane from Oxford, in which he desired " to hold correspondence with him, relying upon his true inclination to the public good and knowing him to have a strong party in the House, and he the chiefe of it."[a] Vane showed the letter to the Speaker of the Commons and to the members of the committee appointed to investigate Riley's plot, and it was agreed amongst them that Lovelace's proposal should be accepted. Vane wrote in reply to Lovelace, and sent the chaplain of the Earl of Warwick, Mr. Wall, to have an interview with him at Henley.[b] The matter was first brought before the notice of Parliament in consequence, as it appears, of Essex discovering that communication was being held with the enemy. On Jan. 17 he complained to the House of Lords that letters were passing between Sir Henry Vane and Lord Lovelace, and that unless the correspondence was put a stop to he could not

[a] Whitacre's Diary, *Additional MSS.* 31116, fol. 108b.
[b] Whitacre's Diary, *Additional MSS.* 31116, fol. 109a; C. J. p. 369.

discharge his duty as general.[a] The same day the Speaker of the Commons gave information to the House of what had passed. The letter written by Lovelace from Oxford, Vane's reply, and the account given by Wall of his interview with Lovelace, were read and then delivered to the Speaker, " to be kept by him from public view." [b] The matter, however, did not rest here. Lovelace, either before or after this date, wrote to Vane from Reading, and Vane again replied.[c] The bearer of a letter written by Lovelace was arrested on Jan. 18 as a spy and examined by Dorislaus, the advocate of the army. His answers led to the examination of Wall on the 19th, and the answers of Wall to the examination, on the 20th, of a third man, Mr. Sterry, who was chaplain to Lady Brooke.[d] The names of Vane and of other members of Parliament appeared in the examinations, and a report got abroad that Vane was under arrest, and that he and other members of the Commons were, in accordance with an ordinance of Parliament, going to be tried by a court of war for holding correspondence with the enemy.[e] Vane complained in the Commons that the privileges of the House had been broken, because witnesses had been examined with regard to the actions of its members without communication having first been made to the House (Jan. 24).[f] Essex received an order to send the examinations to the House, with which he complied, at the same time declaring through Strode that he had never thought of causing any members of Parliament to be tried by martial law.[g] He also in person presented copies of the examinations to the

[a] L. J. p. 381.   [b] C. J. vol. iii. p. 369.

[c] Whitacre's Diary, Additional MSS. 33116, fol. 110b.

[d] C. J. vol. iii. p. 376.

[e] Whitacre's Diary, Additional MSS. 31116, fol. 110b ; King's Pamphlets, The Kingdom's Weekly Intelligencer, E. 18/8.

[f] Whitacre's Diary, Additional MSS. 31116, fol. 110b.

[g] C. J. vol. iii. p. 375.

House of Lords, which ordered the Speaker to give him thanks for his care, and declared that he had done nothing but what was in accordance with his duty as Lord General.[a] The Commons, on their side, proceeded to summon before them and question Dorislaus. After a long debate they appointed a committee to examine the matter further and to report whether in its opinion a breach of privilege had been committed or not.[b]

The letters which passed between Lovelace and Vane are not printed in the Journals of either House; but there is no doubt, with regard to their contents, that offers made to Vane, as chief of a large party in the Commons, would include some general promise of religious toleration.[c] It does not appear whether Lovelace wrote at Bristol's instigation; but, according to Wall's report, he acted with the authority of the King.[d] It was natural that some other agent than Ogle should be employed to approach Vane, in order to preclude danger of the discovery and betrayal of the designs upon Windsor and Aylesbury. Charles by making propositions to Vane, if he did not succeed in much, at least succeeded in nearly involving the two Houses in a quarrel over a question of privilege. The Houses, however, could not afford to quarrel. Two days after Essex delivered up the examinations Parliament was informed of Ogle's conspiracy, and the ill-timed dispute

---

[a] L. J. vol. vi. p. 391.

[b] L. J. vol. iii. p. 376. Whitacre's Diary, *Additional MSS.* fol. 111a.

[c] The weekly papers only mention the affair slightly. *Anti-Aulicus* gives as follows the contents of Lovelace's letter to Vane :—" That the King having taken notice of him and of others of his judgment, and conceiving them to be reall and hearts in their intentions, did promise unto them liberty of conscience, and that all those laws that have been made by the parliament, and all others, the rights and liberties of the people, should inviolably be preserved : of which hee would give what assurance could be devised ; desiring likewise that either hee or some other by his appointment would upon safe convoy treat further of the business at Henley, or what other place he thought fit."—*King's Pamphlets*, E. ⁴⁴.

[d] Whitacre's Diary, *Additional MSS.* 31116, fol. 108b.

appears to have been abandoned, since no further notices of it are to be found in the Journals. On Jan. 26 Lord Wharton reported to the House of Lords:—

A discovery of dividing the two kingdoms of England and Scotland, and the design of the betraying of Alsebury, the effect whereof was to this purpose :—That Devenish, the keeper of Winchester House, was dealt with to permit Captain Ogle to make an escape out of his custody, which the said Devenish discovered to some Lords ; and the moderate men (as they called them) and the Independents were to join together for suppressing of the Presbyterians, and the Scots to be kept out of the kingdom ; and Ogle had an hundred pounds sent him from the Earl of Bristoll to bear his charges out of town. And further, the Earl of Bristoll dealt with one Mosely to surrender the garrison of Alsebury ; and in case the King's forces could not have the town surrendered them, to fire it and the magazine.

Four documents,[a] according to the entry, were then read, after which,

Lieutenant-Colonel Moseley was called into the House and thanked for his fidelity and good service done at Aylesbury for the Parliament : who acquainted the Lords, " That he had been dealt withall from Oxon to have blown up the magazine at Aylesbury and some part of the town, with two engines sent from Oxon, whilst their forces should have surprised the said town." [b]

Upon the further report of Lord Wharton, " that Mr. Nye and

---

[a] (1) Ogle's letter to Bristol, dated Nov. 24 (No. 1). (2) The King's letter to Lieutenant-Colonel Mosely concerning the surrendering up to him the town of Aylesbury (missing). (3) The King's letter to Thos. Devenish, keeper of Winchester House, dated from Oxford, 12 Jan. 1643 (missing). (4) The Propositions (No. 2).

[b] *The Scottish Dove* (E. $\frac{4}{8}$) gives the following account of Mosely's share in the business: " There having lately been some difference of discontent between Lieutenant-Colonel Mostley and some other commanders, the Lieutenant, coming to London upon his occasions, was closed with by some Oxford factors (for treachery), and, after much sifting, the Lieutenant-Colonell carrying the business smoothly, the bargain came to be confirmed, and 1,000 pound must be the reward to deliver up Alesbury; the place was appointed where and how to agree of the time and way, to which place, according to promise, Lieutenant Mostley sent his man. The time being appointed, he desired money in hand; 100 pound was sent him, a good horse and a sword; and on Monday [1] they came to have possession. But Lieutenant-Collonell Mostley, when he had the 100[li] had all he looked for, and had made the business known to the governour." [2]

---

[1] They marched Sunday night, Jan. 21-22.
[2] Colonel Aldridge, *The Weekly Account*, E. $\frac{3}{1}$.

Mr. John Goodwin did refuse to meddle in the business," the House—

thought fit that they should have thanks given them from the House for the same ; and that Lieutenant-Colonel Mosely and Mr. Devenish should have thanks given and a reward for their faithfulness in the carriage of this business.—(L. J. vol. vi. p. 395.)

The same day, January 26, at the request of the Lords, a conference by committees of both Houses was held in the Painted Chamber. In the report of the conference afterwards made in the Commons the House was informed :

That Ailesbury was much in the King's eye; that Mr. Devenish was very faithful to the Parliament, and in discourse in the whole proceeding of this business; that he got Ogle to pawn his seal unto him; and thereby got a new seal cut, and opened Ogle's letters, and sealed them with the new seal. That Mr. Goodwyn, Mr. Nye, with the privity of my Lord General and some members of this House, had conference with Ogle. That the King's forces came on the Sabbath day[a] last towards Ailesbury; and his forces at Tocester quitted that garrison in hopes of effecting this design. That three hundred fresh foot were sent on that day by his Excellency into the town; of which notice was given by Lieutenant-Colonel Mosely to his Majesty to defer it a few days; but, indeed, to the end, to defer the time, till my Lord General and the Earl of Manchester's forces might march between the enemy and Oxford: yet it so much concerned his Majesty to have that town delivered on that day, in regard of upholding his reputation with his Parliament at Oxford, who were to meet the next day, that he would defer the time no longer; but, in the great storm and snow, marched within two miles of the town; and near four hundred men lost in the march.[b]

---

[a] Jan. 21.

[b] The following is the list of documents entered in the Commons' Journals as being read to the House; several are not in the Tanner Collection, while several in the Tanner Collection are not entered in the Journals. The clerk does not appear to have had regard to order of date:—

(a.) A Letter from Captain Ogle, prisoner in Winchester House, to the Earl of Bristol.

(b.) Propositions of peace.

(c.) A Safe Conduct under the King's hand with a blank of three names.

(d.) The Earl of Bristol's letter to Lieutenant-Colonel Mosely.

(e.) Lieutenant-Colonel Mosely's Letter to the Earl.

(f.) Mr. Devenish's Letter to the Earl of Bristol.

(g.) The King's Warrant to Mr. Devenish to set Captain Ogle at liberty.

The Commons, after hearing the report, resolved that thanks should be returned to Mr. Nye, Mr. Goodwin, Lieutenant-Colonel Mosely, and Mr. Devenish, and that the estate of Mr. Samuel Crispe should be forthwith secured. With regard to the main question both Houses dwelt as lightly upon it as possible, and sought to show that the King, when making promises to the Independents, had no other design in view than to foment discord and gain military advantages for himself. The following resolution was adopted by both Houses: " That it doth appear, upon the whole matter, that the King and his council at Oxford do endeavour and embrace all ways to raise and foment divisions betwixt us and our brethren of Scotland, and amongst ourselves, under the fair pretence of easing tender consciences; that during these fair pretences, their immediate design was the ruin of the kingdom by the destroying and burning of the magazines thereof." [a]

What is here quoted from the Journals is all that was ever officially made known. None of the documents were printed or published, and the weekly papers either do not notice the affair at all or pass lightly over it. [b] The Weekly Intelligencer, which has the fullest

(*h.*) Mr. Devenish, his Letter by Captain Ogle to the Earl of Bristol, in figures.

(*i.*) The Earl's Answer to Mr. Devenish.

(*k.*) The King's Warrant to Mr. Devenish to raise two hundred men under his son's command, to be put into the garrison of Windsore.

(*l.*) The Earl of Bristol's letter, in figures, to Mr. Devenish.

(*m.*) Sir George Strode's Letter to Mr. Samuel Crispe to pay one hundred pounds to Captain Ogle.

(*n.*) The Bill of Exchange for the payment of the said hundred pounds.

(*o.*) Mr. Samuel Crispe's Letter to Sir George Strode.

(*p.*) Captain Ogle's Letter to Lieutenant-Colonel Mosely, about the time of delivering up of the town.

(*q.*) His Majesty's Instructions to Lieutenant-Colonel Mosely to blow up the magazine in case of sudden discovery.

The engines or fireworks delivered by his Majesty's own hands for the said service was presented likewise to the House.

[a] C. J. vol. iii. p. 378.

[b] *King's Pamphlets: the Parliament's Scout*, E. ⅗ ; *Anti-Aulicus*, E. ⅔; *The Kingdom's Weekly Intelligencer*, E. ⅒.

account, dwells entirely on the military side of the negociation. The writer mentions some details which are not in the letters that we possess, and it is likely enough that he drew upon his imagination for some of them.ᵃ The chief portion of his narrative is as follows:

> After some debate, Ogle could not accomplish his ends unless he might have his liberty. . . Master Devenish did wisely connive at his escape, Lieutenant-Colonel Mosely nobly entertained him at Aylesbury, and concluded on conditions to deliver up the town ; Ogle went to Oxford, kissed his Majesties hand. . . . Hereupon his Majestie writes a letter, and the Earl of Bristol another, to Lieutenant-Colonel Mosely, and also to Mr. Devenish, and thanks them for their affection to his Majesties service. Mr. Devenish writes a letter of compliance to the Earle of Bristol, and also sends him a figure to write by, but yet advises his Lordship that Ogle may not be privy to what he writes, for he loves to be free with solid and reserved men—of either of which Ogle was never guiltie. My Lord Bristol accepted of the figure, answered it in kinde, approved of Mr. Devenish's advice, sent him a letter of indemnity under his Majesties hand and seal for permitting Ogle to escape, intimating unto him that his Majestie had made Ogle a gentleman of his privy chamber, but a badge of greater honour was intended for him. Mr. Devenish finding his addresses so acceptable, writ againe in figures to the Earle of Bristol, and propounded unto him a designe he had to betray Windsor Castle at the same time into his Majesties hands by taking advantage of a feare that would possess them upon the surrender of Aylesbury. His Majesty and the Earl of Bristol well approved of the designe, and both of them in several letters signed with their own hands highly extolled his wisdom, promised great rewards, as by the letters · appear.
>
> The plot goes on; Sunday, Jan. 21, at 12 at night, Aylesbury was to be delivered up; to that end his Majesty quits Tocester,ᵇ and draws all the forces he can also from Oxford and elsewhere to enter Aylesbury: Lieutenant-Col. Mosely sends his Majesty word that there was come in three full companies of foot, fresh supplies, which he expected was sent upon some jealousies, therefore advised his Majesty to forbear to send till a better opportunity: but his Majesty was resolved on the time appointed,

---

ᵃ See No. 23 and note.

ᵇ The Royalists had a garrison at Towcester, from whence they made plundering excursions into the surrounding districts. A party of Cavaliers took Sir Alexander Denton's house, Hilsdon, within a few miles of Aylesbury, but were driven away by a body of Parliamentarians coming from Banbury and Newport Pagnell about Jan. 17. On Jan. 18 the Royalist forces abandoned Towcester, after which the place was occupied by the Parliamentarians. *The Kingdom's Weekly Post*, E.⁴⁴; *Mercurius Civicus*, E.⁴⁴; *The Scottish Dove*, E.⁴⁴; *Mercurius Civicus*, E.𝖸.

for that the winde had blowne of late much against them, and the great meeting of
the Parliament was at Oxford the next day, and some action must suddenly ensue
to uphold his reputation at so great a meeting, and therefore sent him, by his own
man, some engines to fire the magazine in case he was discovered, that then the
towne might be easily taken by storming it: but when they came within two miles
of Aylesbury [a] the enemy perceived they were betrayed, so retreated in disorder, and
lost neer 400 men and horses in the snow, and lost Tocester besides; and had Lieutenant-Colonel Moseley prevailed to hold off the day of appointment but two days
longer, as he endeavoured it, my Lord General's forces had marched between Oxford
and the enemy, and cut them off, but unseasonableness of the stormes and wayes
were such that they could not march but with much prejudice, though they endeavoured it.[b]

Notice should be drawn to the peculiar use of the word
" agitations," on p. 1, which may help to explain the use of the
word " agitators " for the agents appointed by the soldiers in 1647.

[a] " The enemy quartered at Ethrop House within two little miles of Alesbury,
expecting the prize; but by the next morning by some scout or secret intelligence
they had notice that their plot was blasted, so they returned back towards Oxford."
—*The Scottish Dove, King's Pamphlets*, E. ⁴⁸⁄₉.

[b] *King's Pamphlets: The Kingdom's Weekly Intelligencer*, E. ⁴⁸⁄₉. The weather
was very inclement, and the operations of the forces on both sides impeded in
all parts of the country.

A SECRET NEGOCIATION WITH CHARLES I.

(1.) THOMAS OGLE TO THE EARL OF BRISTOL.

[Tanner MSS. vol. lxii. fol. 332.]

MY LORD,

Having by God's great marcy bin soported by his great provydenss (after almost 7 months most myserable close improsinment, aggravated with most exquiset acts of barbarissme and cruelty, in the Lo: Petter's[a] howse, and from thenss 20 days in the hoolr of a ship) obtayned (not through favour but forgetfulnes of these grand refformers) the lyberty of Winchester Howse, where now I am a prisner, som of my freinds and aqueyntans had recorss to me, wherby my former agitations (well known to Sir Nich. Crisp)[b] for

---

[a] Petre's.

[b] Sir Nicholas Crispe, a royalist, a former farmer of the customs, who had fled from London to Oxford in the beginning of the year. On Jan. 18, 1643, several intercepted letters were read in the House of Commons ; amongst others, one from Sir Robert Pye, an Exchequer officer, whose son Hampden's daughter had married. In this letter Sir Robert Pye "shewed that hee had paied 3700ll due to Sir Nicholas Crispe for secrett service done for his Matie, and would take a course to convey his Maties revenue to him."[1] The money lent by Crispe to the King, Whitaker, in his *Diary*, informs us, was part of the money due to the Commonwealth for customs.[2] When questioned, Pye declared that he was entirely ignorant of the service for which the money was paid to Crispe, who was summoned before the House, "and ther answered, that this 3700ll was due to him from his Matie for monies advanced when his Matie went against the Scotts, which afterwards appeared to be a manifest lie by his often

---

[1] D'Ewes' Diary, *Harl. MSS.* 164, fol. 277a.

[2] *Additional MSS.* 31116, fol. 29b.

CAMD. SOC.   B

the advansing his Mag[t] seuviss did not only revive, but upon the passing the Scots Covynant my former hops and assuranss to add to his Mag[t] the most considerable part of the people heere were doubled; who as formerly they boothe insenced and mayntayned the warr against his Mag[t], so now are they censerly [a] desyrous to ther utmost to assist his Mag[t] for sopresing this Covynant and the mylisha, som humble desyes of thers for ther assuranss of injoying the benyfet of his Mag[t] vehement prodistations and gratious declorations, being granted by his Mag[t] (as an earnist thereof) for the beter setlement and inabling them with his Mag[t] asistans to tourne the streame, to which work they are only led through contiens towards God, devotion to his Mag[t], and compasion to the bleeding state of ther native contry.

To intymate which to his Mag[t] they have made use of me, bothe in regard of my former addresses to, and also sopossing that my long and great sufferings for his Mag[t] has begot me confydenss and credit at Coort, and lastly in cace of any myscoradg or discovry heerof they know themselvs safe in my hand, wherfore I have made bould to certyfy your honor, being well assured of your fydelity to his Mag[t], our Church and State, and also knowing your wisdom to

uncertaine and almost contradictorie answeares; soe as wee all concluded that this monie had been lent his Ma[tie] since his departure from the cittie of London, though the said Sir Nicholas Crispe absolutelie denied, being asked the question by the Speaker; yet awhile after hee slipt away from the doore of the Commons house and went to his Ma[tie] to Oxford, which easilie cleared the scruple, when the saied monie had been lent for secrett service." [1] After this the Commons ordered all the goods of the offender to be seized, Jan. 20.[2] The following day Colonel Manwaring, appointed to search the houses of Sir Nicholas Crispe at London and at Hammersmith, to see what money or plate could be found there, made his report, "but of 300[li] that was found in his house; but he found of gold of his in the Tower, and in other places of the city, to the value of neare about 5000[li]; all which was seized, because he had slipt away out of the sergeant's custody, and was not to be found."[3]

[a] Sincerely.

[1] D'Ewes' Diary, *Harl. MSS.* 164, fol. 277a, b; C. J. vol. ii. 933.
[2] C. J. vol ii. 936.
[3] Whitacre's Diary, *Additional MSS.* 31116, fol. 21b.

manadg the greatest affayre aright. What the particulore passages betwixt Sir Nich: Crispe and me were I shal not trouble your Lodship with, he being at Oxford, and able to give your honor a full and satisfactory acoumpt thereof, only thus much upon thes proposisions to me. I then tould him it was not possible to setle the comision of array in London untal som reall acts were don by his Mag^t to satisfye the people (who would not be satisfyd with words) of the reality of his Mag^t performanss according to his prodestations and declarations, which corrs, if it had bin then taken, I may without bouldnes or vanity afferm to your Lodship that the warr had bin ended, a ferme peace and confydenss of his Mag^t defending the Protestant religion, the laws and libertys of the kingdom, and governing heerafter by the known laws, had bin most assuradly setled in the people. And if it please God this overture be now axeptable to his sackred Mag^t and your Lodship it wilbe a notable evydenss that the blessing of God is with us, and that this land is not designed for ruen, which heer is more confydently beleved, because his sackred Mag^t having sene the myschefous evels of two extremitys, the goulden meane is to be laboured for, which is obtayned only by moderat not violent corses and counsels.

The only thing desyred for present, is a safe conduct for two or three who on the behalf of many thousands may com to Oxford, and propound ther humble desyrs to his Mag^t, and receve such satisfaction and derections conserning the further prosecution thereof, as to his Mag^t and your Lodships wisdom shall seeme meete; for the better effecting heerof I have sent inclosed the effect of what is intended, to be presented to his Mag^t at ther comming to Oxford, with the circomstanses, grounds, and reasons of the same, whereby your Lodship may the bettor facilytate the work and guide them and me aright therin.

The party heer that have insenced and mayntaynd this warr consists of 3 sorts of people, the fyrst and greatest are the moderat zelous prodistants, lovers (though desyrous of som amendment) of the Comon Prayer booke. The second and next considorable to this are the rigid Presbyteryans; the third are the Independants and Brownists, among whom doe some few and very inconsiderable anababtists and other fantastick sectuarys myx themselvs. Thes 3 though realy ayming at sevrall ends for ther speritual, yet ther temporall intrests being one and the same, and conseving Episcopasy and the prorogative were the only obsticle to ther desyrs in both, and the way either to remove or abate this were only by this parlament, did joyne together to soport the means against this soposed enemys; evry one cherishing themselvs in ther several hops and wishes for the injoyment of ther freedom in the exersise of ther devotions; whylst they knew they did unanimosly agree for the security of ther outward estats.

And thus the cunning Presbateryan made a real use of both the others power to effect ther owne ends, which they never aymd at; but now, visably seeing, doe abhor this Scots Covynant, and the rather because thay setle to establish that, they can scarce cal any thing ther owne: hense having recorss to the use of ther reason, they conclud that tis beter for them to live under episcopasy, injoying the benyfyet of his Mag^t frequent prodistations and gratious declarations, than under the terany of the mylisia and malisious Presbyteryan; upon which grounds both thes partys begin to stager, and repent of ther formore actions; and if his Mag^t as a gratious father will reseve thes prodygall children, they will not only quyte fall of from thes Covynantors, but visably apere for his Mag^t, which being don, your Lodship easyly sees that the warr will quickly end, the Scots be kept out of the kingdom, and his sackred Mag^t returne home with honor and victory, for what the soule is to the body, so were and are the two to all the actions and opposisons that have bin don and made.

Som of the leading men, both mynisters and others of the fyrst sort, upon passing the Scots Covynant, came to Winchester Howse to me lamenting ther owne and the kingdoms myserys, afferming that the moderat men who at * asisted the parlament to secure themselves and bring in delinkquents would now most willingly not

* Sic. ? had.

only withdraw but assist his Mag^t agst this Presbyteryan warr, if they could be assured of his Mag^t parformanss according to his prodestations and declarations. And the meere dispayre of his Mag^t had drove them and still would inforce them to continew the assistanss contrary to ther desyrs, which were rather for moderated Episcopasy than the Scots Presbitrys, and that the supreme comand of the milisia should continew in the formor antient corss, and not be violently extorted from the crowne.

But in cace ther were, as was affermed, a reall plot to reare Popery and terany upon the ruens of this parlament, then skin for skin, and all that he hath will a man give for his lyfe, how much more for religion, the lyfe of the life, to setle and assure this mene. Thay were assured by Corah and his complyces that popry and terany was both the ends and ayms of al his Mag^t actions, and that ther was no other way to prevent them than a violent alteration of goverment both eclesastycall and civell; for profe heerof ther was a Pops bull found and som victorys [a] sayd to be obtaynd.

The other sort, vid. Independants and Brownists, being more fyry though not more inraged at the Scots Covynant, which wholy blasted ther hops of a toleration or conivanss at the least of the exercys of ther owne disyplyne, mett together, and drue up a very high and daring peticion to the parlament, requyred that the Scots Covynant might not pass, or at least not be pressed upon them, for that thay did not take up arms for the Scots prisbitry, which is as antychristian or more then the Einglish prelacy; if this therfore were not don, they would not fyght themselvs into a worss condision, but the 3 regaments in the army of thes men would lay downe ther arms and the rest withdraw ther assistanss.

The Presbytiryan, seing the mischef and ruen which this petition brought with it, bent all ther indevors to sopress it, and for this end, as thay formerly sent Mr. Nye into Scotland for the cherishing the hops of that faction then, soe now they imploy him agayne to quyet the rage and quensh the fyre of this peticion, giving them

[a] *Sic.* ? miscopied "writings."

assuranss they shall reseve satisfaction and be gratyfyd with what kind of disyplyn ther humors cals for, wherby the peticion was stopt for present.

But yet ther jelosy of the Scots Press[bytery] remayns greater then ther displesur against the Einglish prelat, from whenss coms this ther result of seeking to his Mag^t, from whom if they can obtayne so much favour as the papist eather formorely had or heerafter shal have, thay will realy joyne to the utmost with his Mag^t to sopress the Scots Covynant and the mylisha. Upon thes reasons and grounds, by the advise of som of the princypall men of both syds, this inclosed paper was drawne up, contayning the substanss of ther humble desyrs to his Mag^t with the grounds therof.

Thus have I, Right hono^{ble}, given your Lodship as breifly as I could an acount of what was intrusted unto me, which if it shall prove effectuall to re-establish his Mag^t just power and athority and the peace of this myserable distraced^a Church and State, I shall think myself a most hapie man, to have contrybuted any thing to so pious a work for my most graticus sovoragne and contry, and the rather for that your Lodship (whose esteme next to his Mag^t I am more covytous of then of anys in the world) shall be *opefex*^{b} *rerum et meliorum temporum origo.* And that your Lodship may be the more confydent of suckses I have comision to assure your Lordshipp that his Mag., gratiously satisfying those who shall com under safe conduct in this humble desire, Alsbury will be surendred to his Mag^t in earnist of further parformanss as need shall requyre, and that his Mag^t may not be jelos of any trechory as at Poolr,^{c} ther wilbe

---

^{a} Distressed. ^{b} *Sic.*

^{c} In September 1643, Captain Francis Sydenham, one of the captains of the garrison of Poole, agreed on a certain night, when he should be captain of the watch, to admit the royalist forces, under the Earl of Crawford, into the town. Crawford arrived at the appointed hour with 500 men, and found the gate, as had been promised, left open; but no sooner had some of his force passed through it than they were attacked by the enemy, who were lying in wait for them, and driven out with loss of many arms, horses, and men.—*Rushworth*, part iii. vol. ii. p. 286.

noe more stranth[a] needfull then a comision under the broad seale, whereof that your Lodship may be yet more asured thes letors are safly convayd to your honor, and the answer wilbe as safly returned hither to me, by the countnanss and power by[b] one of the chefe offycers in this garyson.[c]

And for the further assuranss those who originaly began thes overturs and actualy will compleate them, have such power and intrest in the keeper[d] of this prison, that upon his reseving a warant from his Mag[t] for my discharg I shal com along with those who com to Coort under the safe conduct, to the end I may add my best asistanss for a hapie concluson therin.

I shall therfore feaer further to trouble your Lodship at this tyme, hoping shortly to kiss his Mag[t] hand and wayt upon your honor, only desyring your Lodship to dispach this mesinger spedyly (who knows nothing of the contents heerof) with a safe conduct (leaving a space for 3 nams under his Mag[t] riall hand and privy signit, with your Lodship's atestation), and lick'wise a warant so signed and sealed, derected to the keeper of Winchester Howse, for my discharg out of prison. The reason why the safe conduct is desyred with a blank is in chanse this letor should myscary, the nams being conseld, noe man can suffer but myself; at our coming his Magisty and your Lodship shall receve a full acount of the stranth[a] and state of the army.

Thus agayne humbly and earnisly praying your Lodship spedyly to dispach this mesinger, and not to discover to any person save his or hir Mag[t] (who wilbe humbly peticioned to interpose and medyate with his Mag[t] in thir behalf) in any measure or kynd that eather this or any thing of this nature, or of any great importanss is com from London; for tis known som great ons at Court hould corespondanss heere. With my frequent prayers to Almyghty God

---

[a] Strength. [b] *Sic.* ? of.

[c] Lieutenant-Colonel Mosely. *See* No. 4 and notes.

[d] Thomas Devenish, who caused a copy to be made of Ogle's seal, opened his letters, and resealed them with the new seal.—C. J. vol. ii. p. 398.

for al the blesings of this and beter lyfe upon his and hir Most
Sackred Mag[t] and posterity, whom that I may serve in this or any
other thing before I com to Coort, I beg your Lodships instroctions,
making bould to wryt myself, as I realy am, my Lord,

Y[r] Ho: most humble and faythful servant,

TH. OGLE.

Winchester Howse, the 17 of Octo: 1643.

The letter sent was dated 24 Noue. 1643.[a]

Indorsed: Coppy of Ogle's letter to L[d] Bristow, 24 Nove. 1643.

(2.) PROPOSITIONS SENT BY THOMAS OGLE TO THE EARL OF
BRISTOL.

[Tanner MSS. vol. lxii. fol. 324.]

Since its undeniable that nothinge can bee added to the happines
of thys Church and State, if the benefitts proposed and promised
in his Ma[ts] many and frequent protestacions and declaracions,
confirmed and attested by Oathe and Sacrament, can bee reallie
inveyed,[b] and that through diffidence of his Ma[ts] performance and
reallitie this unnaturall civill warre, with all the miseries of the
same, still rageth amongest us, which difference principally is caused
through a beliefe that all these late acts of grace in satissfaction of
the former misgovernement, for prevention of the like in tyme to
come, and for a through reformacion, were compulsivelie and by
constreant, and not voluntarilie and for the compassionate weale of
the subject passed by his Ma[tye]; hence it is that the people beleive
that they cannot safely enjoy religion and lawes by the proffered
reformacion, nor bee free from the former cou[rt][c] incroachments
upon theire soules, bodyes, and estates, by any other meanes then an
utter extirpacon and allteracon of Episcopalle governement, which
haveinge a strength in and uppon the civill power, and by diver-

---

[a] Information given by the copyist. [b] *Sic.* ? injoyed.
[c] This may stand for " court " or " covert."

sion weakeninge his Ma^{ts} auctoritie his Ma^{tye} is necessitated to defend the same, from whence ariseth the bloodie quarrell of the militia. To settle therfore a confidence in the people of his Ma^{ts} reallitie in mayntenance of religion, the just priviledges of parliament, the lawfull libertie and propertie of the subject, and his future government by the knowne lawes of the land, without the alteracon of Episcopalle governement, and the trust of the militia reposed in the Crowne.

1. Theese meanes are heartilie proposed and desired that his Maiesty wilbee gratiously pleased to consent unto, and that all the ould Bishopps, what have brought in and practised the late innovations in the Church, whoe have tyranised and oppressed his Ma^{ts} subjects in theire severall judicatures, bee forthwith displaced, and that his Ma^{tye} choose the ablest and most consciensious divines, whoe through theire unblameable livs and doctrine have interest in the peoples affections, in theire steade.

2. That his Ma^{tye} doe graunt out a commission as was doune 1mo Elizabeth, to certeyne visitors for regulateing of ceremonies, and appointinge certeyne orders in the Church untill a free, nationall, and right composed Synod can bee called for setlinge the distractions of the Church, whoe may ymediatelie pull doune all allters, superstitious pictures, and prohibitt the practise of the former innovacons, as boweinge to or towards the allter att the name of Jesus, standinge att *gloria patri*, and the diviscon of service, etc.

3. That a proclamacion bee forthwith published, as *in primo Hen.* 8^{rl}, that all those whoe have byn oppressed in the former misgovernemenʈ shall* uppon theire repaire to Court shalbee* with all speade repaied and the oppressors punished according to justice, that thereby the world may see his Ma^{tye} will doe justice against the Bishopps and the culpable ceremonious abettors, that the warre is not mainteyned for defendinge delinquents from due punishment.

4. That all delinquents accused both by his Ma^{tye} and the two

* *Sic.*

Houses bee tryed either by a knowne lawe, or in a full and free Parliament, or that his Majestie bee pleased to graunt such a generall and free pardon as by the advise of the two Howses of Parliament may secure all men's feares.

5. That his Ma^{tye} bee pleased to pass such an acte of parliament as the two Howses shall advise for the repaireing the breach of priviledges in his courte* to the House of Commons and secure the Howses from the like hereafter.

6. That his Majestie bee gratiouslie pleased to graunt a safe conducte and give audience to some whoe shalbee appointed to attend his Ma^{tye} by many thowsands of inhabitants in and about London, to propose to his Ma^{tye} the humble desires of the rest comeing for easeinge of theire consciences from such heavye burdens as have byn layd uppon them by Byshopps, and for givinge them assurances for enjoyinge theire freedome from such oppressions and penalties, submittinge themselves unto and obeyinge and mainteyninge his Ma^{tye}, the lawes of the land, of the kingdome in all civil affaires.

Indorsed: Propositions from Ogle to Ld Bristoll, sent with letter to Ld Bristoll, 24 Novem: 1643.

(3.) LIEUTENANT-COLONEL MOSELY TO THE EARL OF BRISTOL.

[Tanner MSS. vol. lxii. fol. 418.]

Though my man be so trusty as I dare commit my life unto his hands, yet the ever watchfull eyes of my enemys are soe over all my actions that I conceive it very dangerous to send him often unto your Lordshipp, which consideration had more startled me, had not he informed me that it was your honour's expresse command

---

* *Sic.* ? coming.

that he should attend your Lordshipp on this Thursday.[a] Yet I question not (if any jealousy should arise by any misfortune) but I should be able so to bleare their eyes as that noe degree of discovery should followe; and I wish my ability to expresse the zealous affection I have to the peace of this kingdom and the prosperity of his sacred Ma[ty] were such as could answere all objections your Lordshipps not knowing me can possibly suggest to your thoughts; for then I should rest assured of your favour in a speedy returne of the signification of his M[ties] and your Lordshipps will concerning the busines in hand. But I knowe the matter requires most serious deliberation, though the agents in it heere even faint with expectation of the issue. I need not trouble your Lordshipp with a declaration of my particular condition; my servant informs me he hath informed your Lordshipp thereoff, only thus much I humbly beseech your honour to know from me, that I accompt myself only happy in this world in being made an instrument capable of doing his M[ty] and the kingdome service. My Lord, my man told me your Lordshipp signified unto him that he which should have been the prime actor in this busines is nowe a prisoner with us, which I am not a little sorry for.[b] Mr. D.[c] (who is a very friend of mine, and he which ingaged me in this service) with myself (as privy therunto) had a way to procure the liberty of my L. Mack Mahoone,[d] and had accomplished our designe had not the tumultuous spirits of some citizens crossed

---

[a] Mosely was at Aylesbury at the time he wrote this letter, indorsed Dec. 6, which was a Wednesday. "This Thursday" would therefore mean the following day, Dec. 7. He went to London about the 9th, "taking with him Bristol's reply (No. 4) to his letter, and also other documents (Nos. 5, 6, 7, 8, 9) received from Oxford on the 8th or 9th, connected with the proposals made by Ogle in his letter of Nov. 24. See No. 14 and note.

[b] As appears from Bristol's reply (No. 4), the person on whom he had his eye was Thomas Ogle. But Mosely is either not aware of this, or affects not to be so.

[c] Devenish, the keeper of Winchester House, as appears from Bristol's reply (No. 4).

[d] The allusion is obscure. Lord Maguire and Hugh MacMahon, both of whom had taken part in the conspiracy to surprise Dublin in Oct. 1641, were at this time

our desire by complaining to the house of his remove (I question
not but your Lordshipp hath heard thereof), whereuppon he was
committed close prisoner to the Tower; yet our designe goes on and
I hope will shortly come to good effect.   If we may doe any service
in the like kinde for the person your Lordshipp means (whom I
cannot guesse) upon the least intimation from your Lordshipp we
shall be as active as possible.   I know not whether your Lordshipp
be acquainted with Major Ogle that sent yow the letter by my hand;
if not, Sir Nic. Crispe can informe your Lordshippe of him; he is a
man of a very working braine, and may possibly doe good service,
[*Last words obliterated.*]   JOHN MOSELY.

Indorsed : L.-Col. Mosely to Lord Bristow, 6 Dec. 1643.

(4.) THE EARL OF BRISTOL TO LIEUTENANT-COLONEL MOSELY.

[Tanner MSS. vol. lxii. fol. 419.]

For yourself.

Though the party you send to[a] be a stranger to you, as as[b] likewise to him,[c] I made the last addresse by this messenger, yet both
your desires seeme to be so reall for the procureing of peace and

prisoners in London.   In May 1643 they had been removed from the Tower to New-
gate.   On Oct. 13 there is the following notice in the *Commons' Journals:*

"Mr. Corbett reports the examination of the business concerning Colonel Read,
Macquire, and MacMahon; the endeavour used to procure their escape.

"Resolved, &c. that the Lords Macquire and MacMahon shall be committed to
the Tower, and kept close prisoners there."   MacMahon, one of the chiefs of the
sept of the MacMahons in the county of Monaghan, may have been spoken of in
London as Lord MacMahon.   He was condemned of treason, and executed at
Tyburn in 1644."—C. J. vol. iii. p. 297.   *A Contemporary History of Affairs in
Ireland*, edited by J. T. Gilbert, vol. i. part. ii. p. 563.

[a] Bristol himself.   [b] *Sic.*

[c] The meaning of this passage is not clear and has probably been mis-copied.
The " him " may perhaps have been originally followed by " to whom," and so refer
to Ogle.   It can hardly refer to Bristol himself, because the words " both your
desires " point to a third person.

quietness in the Church and kingdome that yow shall finde all the assistance and incouragement he can give unto yow. And to the purpose heere goeth a very punctual and exact dispatch of all things that can be desired,[a] the delivery whereof (with safty and speed) is earnestly recommended unto yow, neither can yow employ your paines in a better errand. For the close prisoner you mention in your letter, and for whose release you make the kind offer, it was spoken to your servant that he might conceive that the letters he brought were only for the inlargment of a prisoner, but the prisoner is the Major[b] yow write of. Mr. D. (if it be meant by one Mr. Devonish, of Dorsetshire) if he be hearty and trusty therein the busines will be the better liked of, for that he is knowne (by the party that writeth this) to be an able and dextrous man. If the busines on that side be carried prudently and calmly it shall not here want secrecy nor assistance. Finde meanes (as soone as posibly yow can) of advertiseing of the safe comming of this dispatch to the partyes yow know of; let both yourself and all others (that shall have a hand in this good work) be confident to finde cleere and reall proceeding.

Examined to bee a true coppy of the letter to L. C. M. 11th Dec. 1643, by us,

[c]P. WHARTON.
GILBERT GERARD.
JOHN CLOTWORTHY.

Dec: 7, 1643.

---

[a] Ogle's letter of 24 Nov. and the Propositions reached Oxford Dec. 2. *See* No. 8.

[b] Ogle.

[c] This is the first of the documents to which Wharton, Gerard, and Clotworthy affixed their signatures. Mosely, no doubt, showed them a copy that he or some other made of his letter, written to Bristol from Aylesbury (No. 3), but they could not attest its genuineness. The fact that their names do not appear on the copies of Ogle's letter to Bristol of Nov. 24, and the inclosed Propositions (Nos. 1 and 2), suggest the inference that they did not see the original documents but only copies of them.

(5.) ROYAL WARRANT TO THOMAS DEVENISH.

[Tanner MSS. vol. lxii. fol. 429.]

CHARLES R.

Whereas you have under your custodye att Winchester Howse the person of William* Ogle, gent. detayned prisoner there. Our will and pleasure is [and we] doe heereby strictly charge and commaund you upon sigt heereof to release and sett att full libertye the person of the sayd William Ogle, gent. Of this yow must nott fayle, as you will aunsweare the contrary att your perill, and for soe doeing this shall bee your sufficient warrant. Given under our hand and signett att our court att Oxford this 6th of Decemb. in the ninetenth yeare [of] our raigne.

By his Ma^{tys} commaund,
GEORGE DIGBYE.

To   Devenish, keeper att the
   present of Winchester Howse in Southwarke.

Examined to bee a true coppy this ii^{th b} of Decem. 1643, by us,

P. WHARTON.
GILBERT GERARD.
JOHN CLOTWORTHY.

(6.) SIR GEORGE STRODE TO SAMUEL CRISPE.

[Tanner MSS. vol. lxii. fol. 434.]

COZEN,

Monies doth grow scarce with us, having lyen heere long with wyfe and chyldren (although not soe many as God sent me); my meanes is kept and taken from mee, and my rents detayned. Tho. Greene, of this cytty, will pay me 100^{li} on a noate of soe much paid in London, unto Mr. William Ogle, who I know not. I have

* The name "William" was inserted in mistake for "Thomas." *See* No. 12.
b *i. e.* 11th.

geiven him a byll at syght which I prey see punctually paid, and,
God willing, your said 100[li] shall be repaid yow, with dammages;
but yow may not fayle to pay my byll, my credite resting theron,
which is all wee have left to subsist by. I shall neede say noe
more. Your brother[a] is well in the west, from whom I have a
letter this morning. Restinge

Y[r] kinsman to serve you,
GEOG. STRODE.

Oxon, the 7° x[br], 1643.

Brother Samuell, I pray pay this 100 pownd for S[r] Gorg Strod.

ANN CRISPE.[b]

For my honored kinsman Mr. Samuell Crispe, at the twoe
Black boys in Breed streete, these present, for London.

Examined 11th 10[bris], 1643.

P. WHARTON.	JOHN CLOTWORTHY.
GILBERT GERARD.	OLIVER ST. JOHN.

(7.) BILL OF EXCHANGE INCLOSED IN A LETTER TO OGLE FROM
SIR GEORGE STRODE.

[On the same sheet as the preceding,]

FOR MR. SAMUELL CRISPE IN LONDON.

At syght heerof I pray pay this my only bill off exchange for the
some off one hundred powns, unto Mr. William Ogle, gent., and
put it to account, returninge unto mee his discharge for soe much;
the 7° off x[ber], 1643.

Your servant,
GEO: STRODE.

Examined 11th 10[bris], 1643.

P. WHARTON.	JOHN CLOTWORTHY.
GILBERT GERARD.	OLIVER ST. JOHN.

---

[a] Sir Nicholas Crispe.   [b] ? the wife of Sir Nicholas Crispe.

(8.) LETTER OF SIR GEORGE STRODE TO THOMAS OGLE.

[On the same sheet as the preceding.]

FOR MR. W. OGLE.

Your letter of the 24 of November came safely to hand the 2^d of this month, but the party that writeth it is unknown to him to whom it was directed ;^a and the knight^b mencioned in your letter, with whom former correspondence was had, is absent in the west; yet ther appearing therein soe greate a desyre of peace, and the quiett of the Church and kingdom, all is effected that in your said letter is desyred, and is sent, according to your directions therein gieven, by which it will appeare how willingly all motions tending to peace and accomodation have admittance heere ; and that party that makes you this answere^a as hee hath endevoured to satisfy you in these fyrst beginnings, soe shall hee bee most redy to contribute any thing further in his power that may conduce to the ending off these miseries and dystracsions, by which this church and kingdom are made soe unhappy, which he conceiveth (suitable to what you write) can only be effected by ways of moderation and temper; the parties may com and goe,^c most assuredly, and what is don, I conceive, will geive you noe dyscouragement.

Dec. 7, 1643.

You must be careful that the bill of exchange and letter of advice ^d together and that it bee dyscreetly carried.

The letter dyrected for Mr. W. Ogle hath bin examined, and what is written on the other side is a true copy theroff together with a byll of exchange inclosed therin.   P. WHARTON.

                                     GILBERT GERARD.

11 Decem: 1643.   JOHN CLOTWORTHY.

Indorsed : Coppy of letters to Ogle and Crispe, with letter of Exchange for 100^{li}. 7 Dec. 1643.

^a Bristol.   ^b Sir Nicholas Crispe. *See* No. 1.
^c Between Oxford and London.   ^d A word lost, the page being torn.

(9.) SAFE CONDUCT SENT BY THE KING FOR THREE PERSONS, WITH A BLANK LEFT FOR THEIR NAMES.

[Tanner MSS. vol. lxii. fol. 437.]

CHARLES R.

Charles, by the grase of God, King of England, etc., to our generals, lieutenant generalls, gouvenours of townes, collonells, captaines, and all other officers and soldiers belonging to any of our armies or garrisons, and to all other whom it may conserne, Greeting, Wheras the three persons heerin named, viz.:

.

are to repayre unto our Court at Oxford about our spetiall affayres, we do by thes present streightly charge and comand you to let them passe freely from place to place unto our Courte att Oxford from our cittye of London without lett or interuption. And of theis our comandes we shall expect a due observance from you and every of you, as you will answre the contrarey at your perille.

This safe conduct untill the tenth of Januari next ensuinge the date hearof.

By his Ma^{ts} commaund,

GEORGE DIGBYE.

Examined this 11th of Decem: 1643, to bee a true coppy by us

P. WHARTON.

GILBERT GERARD.

JOHN CLOTWORTHY.

Safe conduct.

(10.) Mr. Samuel Crispe to Sir George Strode.

[Tanner MSS. vol. lxii. fol. 438.]

Honoured Sir,   London, the 12 December, 1643.

Your letter dated the 7th[a] I have received, and according to your
letter and bill of exchange on me I have paide it on sight the
summe of one hundred pounds, and have take[n] up your bill of
exchange and a reciept for it, of which summe [b] is payde to Mr.
Will. Ogle, as will apeare with acquittance I will send by my cousin
Cox; he tell me will goe this weeke. Sir, heere is a most miser-
able time of trading and no mony to be had from any man allmost
that oweth me mony. I pray God send better time, or else this
kingdome will suffer much. Sir, the halfe of our gould [c] that came
is voted in the house, and saith will pay us againe in March next.
God knowe howe it be performed. We could not help ourself,
being all the gould were in their possession, and as yet we have
none power to recover the other half, but shall. The Parliament
sent it all to the Tower to be guined [d]; we gave the Parliament all
that the company were indebted, and want to pay debt. All would
not serve turne. I pray God to worke in the heart of the parlia-

---

[a] No. 6.   [b] Sic.

[c] Sir Nicholas Crispe, Knight (the brother of Samuel Crispe), formerly a farmer
of the customs, had been found by the committee of the navy to owe to the
State more than 16,000l. On Feb. 18, 1643, the Parliament had ordered that
"the stock and adventure in the Ginny Company," belonging to Sir Nicholas, should
be sequestered in the hands of John Wood, treasurer to the company, towards payment of this debt. On the arrival of a vessel, "The Starre," laden with gold ore,
Wood and the other partners agreed to lend the half for the supply of the wants of
the navy, until it should be shown what part belonged to Sir Nicholas. Accordingly, the two Houses ordered that whatever sums belonged to the said Wood and
partners, over and above the said Sir Nicholas Crispe's part of the stock and adventure, should be repaid to them upon the following 25th of March, out of the
customs collected in the port of London, with allowance of 8 per cent. interest.
2 Dec. 1643.—C. J. vol. ii. p. 326; L. J. vol. vi. p. 321.

[d] Coined.

ment to preserve this kingdome. Sir, I pray remember my service to my Lady and all with. yow. So praying God in his due time to send us a joyfull meeting, so shall ever rest

Your to be commanded,

SAMUELL CRISPE.

To my much honoured kinsman, Sir George Strowde, knight, this present.

Attested to be a true coppy by
JOHN MOSELY.
THO. DEVENISH.

(11.) ACQUITTANCE OF THOMAS OGLE TO SAMUEL CRISPE ON RECEIPT OF £100.

[Tanner MSS. vol. lxii. folio 436.]

The xiith daye of December, 1643.

Receaved the day and yeare above written from the hands of Mr. Samuel Crispe the som of on hundred pound of currant English mony. I say received by me, WILL. OGLE.

Attested by
JOHN MOSELY.
THO. DEVENISH.

Indorsed: Coppy of Ogle's acq. to Crispe.

(12.) THOMAS DEVENISH TO THE EARL OF BRISTOL.

[Tanner MSS. vol. lxii. fol. 450.]

RIGHT HONOURABLE,

Tusday[a] last I received a vissite from two frends of my old acquaintanc, whose erand mad them the better welcom, and for answering both ther expectacons I shall not fayle to contribut.

---

[a] Dec. 13, the day this letter is dated, was Wednesday; Tuesday last would be Dec. 12.

my best endevors; one hath his erand, and the other I hope shall not stay long,[a] which at first I resolved to have performed in silenc on my parte, not presuming to trouble your honour espectially at this time, but my duti and affection to the buysnes (which it concerns), the progresse whereof I apprehend to conduce so much to the publique good, that mad me wilfully repell all reasons that might dissuade me, and adventure to give your Lordshipp this best accoumpt, not only of my readeynis to do servic, but allso of the hopes which I conceave of the suckcesse (ther being so good a foundacon laid) if the maiors[b] zeale doth not in the prevention overballance his prudence, which I hope your wisdom will prevente, and in that hope I humbly tak my leave.

Your honours to be
Commanded in what I may,
D.

London, 13⁰ Decem. 1643.

Concordat cum originali.

ex[r] per Tho. Devenish.

Indorsed: Coppy of letter of Devenish to Ld. Bristoll, 13 Decem. 1643.

(13.) THOMAS OGLE TO THE EARL OF BRISTOL.

[Tanner MSS. vol. lxii. fol. 458.]

MY LORD,

On Munday night last [c] late, I received your honours dispatch, whereby I perceive your Lordship did not remember me. Tis

---

[a] Presumably Mosely and Ogle. Mosely came to London about Dec. 9. Compare (No. 14) Mosely to Bristol. [b] Ogle's.

[c] Dec. 15, the day on which this letter is dated, was Friday; Monday last, therefore, Dec. 11. All the letters, &c. written in Oxford Dec. 7 (Nos. 4, 5, 6, 7, 8, 9) were examined by Wharton, Gerard, and Clotworthy on Dec. 11. We have no letter of that date from Bristol to Ogle, and the word "despatch" does not necessarily imply a letter. Bristol may merely have sent the other letters by a messenger of his own. Ogle probably refers to the opening words of Strode's letter to himself (No. 8).

trew I did not presume of any perticuler interest or acquantance with your honour.   But I was confident that, besides Sir Nicholas his informations, your Lordship would easily call me to mynd when you did but heare of Mr. Smart's [a] cause, to which your honour and my Lord Digby[b] were pious and just freinds, in the respective houses.   But principally the matter conteyned in the letter did emboulden me to presume upon my generall acquantance (begun at Rippon at the pasificatione; and continued since in par[liament] upon occasione of my father's cause) with your honour, to make that addres unto your Lordship, by the happy effectinge whereof I hope with approbatione to be booth knowen and admitted by your Lordship hereafter to be your honours faithfull and trusted freind and servant.

My Lord, on Tusday[c] night last (as this enclosed letter and acquittance will shew) I receved the money, for which I retourne your honour most humble and hartie thanks, with assurance that I will never faile upon occasione to requite soe greate a favour.   And the fulness of your Lordship's retourne shall spedily and really (God willinge) be answered by a faithfull performance of the intimatione given, which I assure your honour is heightned to that degre of resolutione (by his Ma[ties] and your Lordship's effectuall resentment) as ther is more resolved and wilbe actually done then I did hope for before our arrivall at Courtt.   And to give your honour the better ground to assure his Ma[tie] hereoff, I send hereinclosed a letter

---

[a] Peter Smart, a prebendary of Durham Cathedral, who, for preaching a sermon against the use of ceremonies, had been degraded from the clerical office by the northern High Commission Court in 1629.   In 1640 Smart brought his case before the notice of the Long Parliament, and Dr. Cosin, who had taken a leading part in his prosecution, was impeached.   As Ogle was Smart's son-in-law it is probable that he came from Durham, where a branch of the Ogle family, of Causey Park, Northumberland, had long been seated.—Hodgson's *History of Northumberland*, vol. ii. part ii. p. 135.

[b] Bristol's eldest son.   [c] Dec. 12.

from Mr. Devenish,[a] whose harte is as right and indeavours wilbe as cordial for establishinge his Maties full, just, and antient power and authoritie, as can be desired. And fore that end he did first ingage the partie who conveyes thes letters, who is most firme, as the effectuall fruites, shortly answeringe your Lordship's expectation and your promise, will evidently declare. Though for the present I am found to delay my cominge (for strengthening our preparations prudently and calmely as your honour advises) thereby to make the event more certayne and infallible; yet within a few weekes your honour may expect us, and I hope shall[b]   *   *   *

My Lord, I besech your honour pardon me for beinge thus generall; the names, the particulers, I am forced to conceale for secrecies sake in case of miscarradge, that whatever becomes of me the busines may happily goe on. And for I have noe more to troble your Lordship with att this tyme, save to desire a few lines to assure me of the receit hereof; and alsoe a kynd and effectuall letter to Mr. Devenish for his and his freinds incouradge-mentt, that his Mag^t will take them into his protectione and satisfy ther disbursements about this busines; with the presentment of my unfeined service to the Right Honourable the Lord Digby, cravinge your honour's pardon and patience, I rest

Your Lordship's faithfull and
Devoted servant till death,
Th. Ogle.

Winchester house,
    X^{ber} 15, 1643.

My Lord, my name was mistake Will. for Thom. Pray pardone my bad wreitinge.

---

[a] Ogle, therefore, inclosed in this letter, dated Dec. 15 (1), Devenish's letter to Bristol (No. 12), dated Dec. 13, and (2) Crispe's letter to Strode (No. 10), dated Dec. 12, which contained his own acquittance for the 100*l*. Mosely was probably the bearer of all at least as far as Aylesbury.

[b] Here follow five words, which I was unable to read with certainty; but they look like " shell a Christenmas pye in it."

Attested a true copy, 15 Dec. 1643,
JOHN MOSELY.
THO. DEVENISH.
Indorsed: Coppy of Ogle's letter to Ld. Bristow, 15 Decem: 1643.

(14.) LIEUTENANT-COLONEL MOSELY TO THE EARL OF BRISTOL.

[Tanner MSS. vol. lxii. fol. 462.]

MY LORD,

I have beene in London these eight or nine daies[a] to get money for the regiment,[b] but have had farre better successe in my more intended busineses. I hope your Lordship doth not thinke it long, when you concider how much it stands us upon as yet (on this side) to be most circumspect, especially my selfe, who having a command am more deeply ingaged both in life and honour should it come to be discovered. My Lord, I delivered the dispatch safely into the person's hands to whom it was directed: the money is paid, the

[a] Mosely probably arrived at London from Aylesbury, Dec. 10 or 11. The papers that he brought with him (Nos. 4, 5, 6, 7, 8, 9) were all read by Wharton, Gerard, and Clotworthy on Dec. 11. On Dec. 12 he visited Devenish. *See* No. 12.

[b] Mosely must have come to London with the double object of getting pay for the garrison at Aylesbury, and of showing the letters which he had received from Oxford. That the Commons were uneasy about the town is apparent from notices in their Journals. The soldiers were unpaid, and threatening to disband. On Dec. 9 there is the following order: "Mr. Browne, Reynolds, Dacres, Fountaine, Sir Jo. Clotworthy, Captain Wingate, Mr. Holland, are presently to go forth to receive informations from the gentleman that is come from Aylesbury, and to consider of some speedy way for the security of that place." Very probably this gentleman was Mosely himself. But, however that may be, it is evident that after his arrival in London the question of finding money for the garrison was recognised to be an urgent one, and that he was not so unsuccessful in his endeavour as he sought to represent.—C. J. Dec. 23, 25, Jan. 8; L. J. Jan. 10.

maior is at his owne will, and intendeth, I thinke, to waite upon your honour the next weeke, unlesse your Lordship upon any service of greater concernement shall command him to stay longer. I percieve their doubtfullnesse, what answer it would please his sacred Matie and your Lordship to give to their motion caused them a little to suspend their activenesse, whereby they are not so fully prepared as I hoped I should have found them; but (may it please your honour) *sat cito si sat bene.* Mr. D. is that Mr. Devenish of Dorset· shire, whose fidelity, discretion, secrecy, and care, I hope your Lordship shall never find cause to question, being a man who (I am persuaded) would spend willingly his dearest blood in opposition of the C[ovenant], which we are all cleare in (and so are thousands in London) will lie heaviere upon us then Episcopacy ever either did or can, which (if his Matie shall please to give a gracious answer to our desires) I question not will be prevented.

My Lord, the only thing I am jealous of is discovery by occasion of my sending to Oxford, both in regard of my many enemies, as also the fate (I thinke) of the towne, which ever hitherto hath had strange successe in discoveries: this doth a litle trouble me, and I should be very happy if your honour would please to give me some direction in it. Many waies have runne in my fancy to secure me; this stratagem doth like me best, if I may have your Lordship's approbation (for without it I will doe nothing). I may pretend to have large proffers made me to deliver up Alesbury to his Matie, which I may discover to my Lord of Essex, and if I can get a warrant from him to treat, *omnis res erit in vado,* I humbly conceive it can be no prejudice to any service to be done (either in that or any other kind) within the spheare of my power; it will worke in them a great confidence of my fidelity, and make them secure of me; and if my servants comming to Oxen be observed, and it come to my Lord Generall's eare, your Lordship knows how I may frame my answer; thus armed I shall be bold to serve his Matie and your Lordship in anything you shall command.

Your honours devoted servant.

Attested to be a true coppy by
JOHN MOSELY.
Indorsed: 18 Dec. 1643, copy of L. C. Mosely to Lord Bristow.

(15.) THE EARL OF BRISTOL TO LIEUTENANT-COLONEL MOSELY.

[Tanner MSS. vol. lxii. fol. 466.]

Your desyres are such for the publicke quiett that yow may be confident of all assistance from hence. Yow goe upon a good grounde and such a one as must unite all honest Englishmen, although in other thinges of different mindes, which is not to be overrunn by an invasion of the Scotts, who if they should prevayle will tyranize both over our estates and consciences.

As for the pretexte you speake of, a way can hardely be sett downe on the suddayne, but use your owne discretion to make such papers and invitations as yow thinke fitt to serve for a pretence uppon any occasion that should happen. But for your going to the Earle you write of, stay a little befor yow resolve on it, untill yow see thinges brought to a little more ripenesse.

Tuesday, at three o'clock, 19th.

Send no oftner then ther is necessity. The party is directed whether to goe privately.*

(16.) THOMAS DEVENISH TO THE EARL OF BRISTOL.

[Tanner MSS. vol. lxii. fol. 494.]

MY LORD,

I hope by this time Ogle is arrived att Oxford.

The contrivance of his passage was soe happyly layde and ordered, thatt noe reflection of prejudice reacheth mee, which in relation to further services I ame nott sorry for.

---

* This letter has no indorsement on it to the effect that it is a copy.

CAMD. SOC.   E

Before hee went wee tasted some, and perticularly Mr. Ny and Mr. Goodwin, whoe as they are very eminent and have great interest in the most active people, soe. wee found them—and theire principles leade them to itt—to bee very desirous of theire liberty. They may proove very instrumentall when they shall have afterwards from the King whatt they may trust too; till when as they will not have sufficient grounds to bee thouroughly satisfyed in theyre owne breasts, soe will they nott engage themselfes with confidence to act upon the cyttysons for soe great an alteration, for if they have nothing to moove them by way of allurement and that all shall be left to theyre jealousy and feare of the Scotch and presbitery, itt may prevayle with them perhapps to retire; but nott to apply themselfes to the King without some reasonable invitations, which these very feares and jealousyes may make way for the embracement of.

By Ogle your Lordship received a character whereof hee hath noe key, because I desire hee should know noe more then your Lordship shall thinke fitt, and for the farther and better prevention of any discovery of this great busynesse of consequence in case of intercepting any lettors. of or on, itt may please your Lordship by your next to commaund mee to whome and whither I shall superscribe my lettors, and your Lordship may bee pleased to direct yours to mee to Mr. Christopher Vine, in Peeter's Streete, in Westminster.

There is a way layde to gitt the names of the officers in the trayne bands of the militia in London, and thatt beeing had, itt shall bee seriously considered whoe will bee the fitter to worke by, and your Lordship shall have an account thereof very speedyly.

Tis conceaved the fitt choyse of persons of severall vocations to bee the first steppe to bee made in this worke, and therefore having already chosen some few of the clergy and of the army (of which I dare boldly reccommend L.-Coll. Mosely as a person of faythfulnesse and ingenuyty) twas thought convenient to make this enquyry into the cytty officers.

The time of the safe conduct will bee exspired the 10th of th[is] instant, and therefore your Lordship will procure and send some of a larger date for three or foure, and yow may bee pleased to cause them to bee single ones, for 'twill be occasion of lesse suspition to have persons goe singly, and there may bee occasion of severall dispatches. However, itt can bee of noe disadvantage to have itt in our choyce.

The bearer heerof is a person whome your Lordship may trust. Hee is (without beeing made acquainted with perticular persons engaged) in some measure made privy into the designe in generall, as one whoe heereafter good use may bee made of, his interest in that sort of people beeing greater then his outward condition promiseth.

Reade to my Ld. Genrall, Sir Gilbert Gerard, Mr. Sollicitor, and examined to bee a true coppy by us this 5th of January, 1643.

P. WHARTON.

THO. DEVENISH.

Indorsed: Coppy of Devenish letter to Ld. Bristow, 5 Jan. 1643.

(17.) THOMAS OGLE TO THOMAS DEVENISH [a]

[Tanner MSS. vol. lxii. fol. 498.]

SIR,

On Weddensday [b] att night last late, I arrived safely here about 9 a cloke, where I found all the portes shutt, but upon informatione thatt I was come by spectiall directions from his Mai^{ty} they were opened and I brought to the partie yow know off, where, after a lardge discourse, his Lordship sent a gent to se me provided for that

---

[a] The words in italics are in cipher, with a contemporary decipher written above them. The MS. is probably a holograph, as it is hardly likely that the copyist would have taken the trouble to copy the cipher. The address on the outside of the MS. and the remains of a seal also suggest that the paper is that which Devenish received.

[b] Jan. 6, the day the letter is dated, was Saturday; Wednesday, Jan. 3.

night, and the next day provisione made of *chambers* in *Mawdlen Colegge* to the end they should be *secretly treated* with all. There is nothing further can be *don in the busines yntil they be*[a] come. Pray therefore in case they *be not*, then *send them hither* with all possible speed, especially Mr. *Nye whom*[b] *yow* may assure to be *admitted his Majesties chaplain and highly preferred* upon the conclusione. Pray therefore faile nott to send Mr. *Nye* to *me*, and lett him make haste hither, as *yow* and *he wish wel to the business.* I have no more to write until we mete, save only that all things are in as good a posture and equipage here as your harte can wish; and in perticuler grea[t] care and respect had of yourselfe, of which yow will assuredly injoye the benefitt in an ample manner ; and so with my harty commendations to yow and your bedfellow I rest your assured

Lovinge faithfull freind,
THOMAS OGLE.

Jan: six[t], 1643.

Addressed: To my honored freind Mr. T. D. att W. in London.

Indorsed: Ogle to Devenish, 6 Janur: 1643.

(18.) THOMAS OGLE TO PHILIP NYE.

[Tanner MSS. vol. lxii. fol. 500.[c]]

SIR,

I hope before my letter come to London to se yow here with me, yet doubtinge ther might be some occasione of longer stay than I expected, 1 did thinke it very necessarie to give an account what truly I find the state here since my short comminge.

[a] "They be" is the correct decipher, though in the MS. an unintelligible word is written.

[b] So by the cipher; the word written is "thom."

[c] The handwriting is the same as in No. 17.

On Weddensday[a] att night last, after the ports were shutt, I came to Oxford, which were commanded by his Matie to be opened upon intimatione that I was there, and after my cominge and stay at court about an hower a lodginge provided for me alsoe, where I made a lardge discourse and received as large a satisfactione as can be desired : which was that those thinges desired should be confirmed, not only by his Matie but by the generall consell[b] appoynted here to mete very shortly, which I assure yow was either caled or at least hastned for this very busines upon my intimatione.

Sir, you are principally loked upon in this busines, and your presence or absence here will mutch hinder or further the effectinge therof. Therfore, since your uttmost endeavers and abilities have bene always bent this way, let nothinge hinder your presence here to attayne the desired end, which is as sincerely intended on this side as it is desired of you. Pray therfore, Sir, make some excuse for your absence for 4 or 5 dayes, as you respect either the cause or your owne preferment, and faile not to come to your very lo. freind to serue you.

THOMAS OGLE.

Directed: *for my reverend friend Mr. Nye one of the assembly* give this in *Westminster,* to his owne hands.[c]

Indorsed : Ogle to Mr. Nye, 7 Janu: 1643.

(19.) HEADS OF INSTRUCTIONS GIVEN BY THE EARL OF BRISTOL.

[Tanner MSS. vol. lxii. fol. 502.]

The demandes in particular.
The particulars that may induce therunto.
That persons be imployed into all places, etc.
That the partyes be hastned away.

---

[a] Jan. 3.　　　　　　　　　　[b] *i.e.* the Oxford Parliament.

[c] The cipher is the same as that used in the previous letter, but is not deciphered in the MS.

L. Say, etc.

Independents wilbe.

Assembly goes on the same grounds.

A disguised hand.

To leave the papers.

[Another hand.]   Direct letters sometimes to Mr. John Squire at Mr. Chesterman's house over against the Crosse Inn in Oxon, and sometimes to M^{ris} Emma Brome at the president's lodgings at Magdalen Colledge.

Indorsed: Ld. Bristoll's Heads of Instructions to the Messenger. 9 Janu: 1643.

(20.) THOMAS OGLE TO THOMAS DEVENISH.

[Copy. Tanner MSS. vol. lxii. fol. 503.]

HONEST FRIND,

Here is inclosed a letter[a] from the Lord that write unto yow. I did mutch admire yow write not to me, and send his letter[b] open that I might understand the contents of it. Pray hereafter let me receive your dispatches, and nothing be concealed from me in this transactione, for it can serve for no end, but to doe great harme, to create jelosies and suspitiones, and to bringe me into a disesteem here: and the mayntenance of my reputatione here wilbe a principall meanes to effect as the means, soe the end, I and yow proposed in this busines. I assure yow I have already met with mighty clashes here, and shall every day have more, if I be discountenanced. Pray therefore send me a coppy of the letter yow sent the partie yow write unto, and me hereafter receive all the dispatches, that therby I may be inabled happily to conclude this busines. I have write to Mr. God.[c] for money. Pray let me have your

---

[a] No. 21.

[b] Devenish's letter to Bristol of Jan. 5 (No. 16).

[c] Mr. Goodwyn. *See* No. 22.

best assistance herein, for I assure yow, upon ther cominge, my repayment of the 100ˡˡ I received will doe them, me, and the busines an extraordinaire advantage and creditt; for as I know yow doubt not my care and fidelitie herein, soe yow need not questione a full, clere, reall, and ingenious dealinge here. This bearer will informe perticulerly of his and my interteynment and conditione here. Ther[fore] I shall write noe more, only dy[sire] yow to hasten them here, to speake to Mr. G. for the money I write for, and let Mr. M. goe to my wife from Mr. G. with the money I mentioned in his letter.

Remember me, and recommend the busines to God in your prayers. *Vale !*

Yr. lo. and assured freind.

9ᵃᵒ Jan. 1643.

Remember Wind[sor ᵃ] and your sone. Ther is somethinge in your letter that seems a contradictione to what I have saide about that busines. Pray avoyde this roke ᵇ here after by your addresses and open letters to me.

Indorsed: Coppy of Ogles to Mr. Devenish, 9 Janu. 1643.

(21.) THE EARL OF BRISTOL TO THOMAS DEVENISH.ᶜ

[Tanner MSS. vol. lxii. fols. 505-508.]

Yours of the 5ᵗʰ of Jan. is come safe to hand, and all things are dispatched according to your desire, and I doubt nott butt the readynesse yow find heere will bee a just ground to begett confi-

ᵃ See No. 23. ᵇ *i.e.* "rock."

ᶜ There are two copies of the Earl's letter. The one partly in cipher, with a contemporary decipher, possibly the paper transmitted to Devenish from Oxford; the other a transcript of the whole, without any cipher. The opening words show that Bristol was writing to Devenish—"Yours of the 5 Jan." (No. 16).

dence, which is the first thing yow must labor to settle, of which this bearar hath instructions to speake with yow. Ogle is heere, and I beleeve will be hearty; yett if itt were nott for the reliance I have upon your discretion and affection in this cause I should nott have those hopes which I have of good successe. I hope God will make yow an instrument of doeing much good and meriting much.

The grounds that in the first place are to bee layd are these:

Thatt men bee induced to unite themselfes agaynst the invasion of the Scots, whose intent can bee noe other then to overrunne this nation.

Thatt men bee convinced in theire judgements that if the presbittery bee once brought in, all sorts of men thatt shall not conforme to them must exspect more severity and persecution in poynt of conscience then from the Spanish inquisition itselfe.

Agaynst this tiranny both over men's fortunes and consciences there must bee an absolute union and conjunction settled in the first place, and this nott onely in London but over all the kingdome of England, thatt the odiousnesse of the Scotts invasion may possesse all true Englishmen's mindes.

In the second place for the securing of the Independents of theire owne ease and liberty, I noe wayes doubt but when the particulars shalbe propounded there will be such satisfaction as will give content to yow or any discreete person or persons that shall be imployed therein. Wherein I most earnestly intreate yow that noe more tyme may be lost, but that some trusty and able parson or parsons be speedily imployd, for it wilbe of greate importance that the buisinesse be in some sort settled before the assembly heere begins the 22th of this month.[a] And as this care is taken for satisfying of Independents, soe they must lay the grounds of the assistance and advantages that may acrew to the King by which he may be induced to this favour and indulgence towards them. And truly it will be expected that those which have above all men bin most active in another way should now be as active in all things that

---

[a] Charles's Oxford Parliament.

may conduce to the King's service, and resisting this wicked invasion of the Scotts, and they must endeavor to make themselves as considerable to the King as possibly may bee.

January 9th, 1643.

Sir John Digby, brother to Sir Kenelme, is in some place prisoner in London. I shal intreate yow to enquire after him and to afford him as much friendship as with discretion yow may, and if. hee should bee in any want I pray yow supply him, and I will see yow satisfyed, and lett him know that yow have such order from mee.

(22.) THOMAS OGLE TO THOMAS GOODWIN.

[Tanner MSS. vol. lxii. fol. 504.]

REVEREND SIR,

This bearer can informe yow what interteinment I and he have had here. And what yow, your brother N.[a] and the rest are like to find; therefore I shall add nothinge, save to desire yow and him, as yow love the cause and your owne contrie and preferment, make haste to me. This bearer can tell yow what I have done in your busines; my care and interest shall not be wantinge to finish itt, which certainly wilbe if yow be not wantinge to yourselfes, for as yow shall receive full satisfactione soe it is here expected that yow give assured testemoneye of your strength and abilities to doe the works proposed; for that end bringe the remonstrance with yow which your brother N.[a] toold me of, and a list of the mil[itia] and com[manders] C[ity] of L[ondon], with an estimate of your strength in booth Ar[mie]s. And alsoe I pray bringe 100[li] or 200[li] alonge with yow, for I am in verie great want of money, etc. Ther is none to be had here to supply either me or themselves. Except, therefore, as I labour in your worke, soe you in some measure assist me to live, and follow it, I cannot continew in this

[a] Nye.

place, but must retire myselfe elsewhere into employment. I know your credit is soe good amongst your con[gregation] that yow may have 200ˡⁱ for askinge. In the meane tyme pray furnish my wife with 40ˡⁱ or 50ˡⁱ, that she spedily come to me with her children. And leave something with her disstressed father [a] towards his releife untill I can take further care for him. This gent. hath promised me the utmost asistance for the procuringe this money. Mr. D. will tell yow wher to find and how to send to my wife. Remember me in your prayers, and make what haste you possibly can to

Your assured lo: faithfull

frind to serve you.

9ⁿᵒ Jan. 1643.

Indorsed : Coppy of Ogles to Mr. Goodwin, 9 Janu. 1643.

(23.) Thomas Ogle to Thomas Devenish.

[Tanner MSS. vol. lxii. fol. 533.[b]   *Undated.*]

Honest Frind,

The newes we received from London of Mr. Roylies and the other committment[c] haith made a stay of my first dispatch. Thes inclosed copies will instruct you sufficientlie of the trew state of that busines and its originall here, which was upon an overture from London by an unknowne man. I conceive its some that I have discoursed unto of the moderate sorte of men, who had not patience to tarry my addres, beinge soe longe delayed. Now your worke is to se if this partie and our correspondents can be joyned firmly together, since the busines is soe sowne brooke outt. Assure yourselfe that ther is

---

[a] *i.e.* Peter Smart.

[b] This letter, and No. 25, are neither dated, signed, nor indorsed. The hand-writing in both is the same, and both, as internal evidence shows, were written by Ogle, the one to Devenish, the other to Mosely. The handwriting is not the same as in Ogle's letters to Devenish and Nye (Nos. 16 and 17). If, therefore, these two last are holographs, Nos. 23 and 25 must be copies.

[c] As Ryley and Violet were committed to the Tower on Jan. 6, it seems most probable that this letter was written before Bristol's letter to Mosely of Jan. 15, and I have, therefore, reversed the order which the two hold in the Tanner MSS.

the most reallytie here can be imagined, soe gratiouse a kinge, soe willinge expressiones he made to me, as would have moved an harte of stone. Pray use your utmost dexteritie to joyne the strenght of booth thes parties together, and be confident of all the helpe and assistance from his Matie thatt can be possiblelie. Upon any way we shalbe advertised, inquire exactly of the busines, the state of itt, and write bake to me in my owne caracter.

I have sent yow a gratious and fre warrant[a] from his Mag^{tie}, who is soe well pleased with your affectiones and the settlementt of the desinge for Windsor before my cominge away, thatt yow may be assured of the benefit. Pray therefore actually and really intend it, and withe all speed settle it accordinge to this warrantt, that att worst will preserve us all, and abate the furie of this presbyterian factione.

The Lord direct us all aright. *Vale* [?]
Your assured faithfull freind.

Pray seind me bake all those papers I left with yow while yow kepe[?] att Westminster. Haste our frind's letter.

---

[a] In the list of documents in the *Commons' Journals* (iii. 378) is mentioned, "The King's warrant to Mr. Devenish to raise 200 men, under his son's command, to be put into the garrison of Windsor." In the *Lords' Journals* (iv. 395) "The King's letter to Mr. Devenish, keeper of Winchester House, dated from Oxford, 12 Jan. 1643." The *Kingdom's Weekly Intelligencer*, No. 41, tells the tale as follows: "Mr. Devenish, finding his addresses so acceptable, writ again in figures to the Earle of Bristoll and propounded unto him a design he had to betray Windsor Castle at the same time into his Majesties hands, by taking advantage of a fear that would possess them upon the surrender of Aylesbury. His Majesty and the Earl of Bristoll well approved of the design, and both of them in severall letters, signed with their own hands, highly extolled his wisdome, promised great rewards, as by the letters appeares." (*King's Pamphlets*, E. $\frac{48}{3}$). The only letter written by the King to Devenish, of which report is made in the *Journals* of either House, is the one mentioned above. We possess only two letters of Bristol's to Devenish, and in one of these (No. 21) there is no mention of a design upon Windsor.

(24) THE EARL OF BRISTOL TO LIEUT.-COLONEL MOSELY.

[Tanner MSS. vol. lxii. fol. 510.]

You are intreated to deferr your journeye and wholy to tende the bussinesse. The tyme holdeth the first day and all thinges wil be readye, according as is settled. You must not fayle to sende your man hether on Friday, to retourne to yow on Saturday,[a] and then advertise the major of all that is further needefull. You may assure your frendes that all goeth here to their mindes, and they and yow I doubt will have much comforte insteede of certeyne distraction otherwayes if Scots prevayle.

This is written by my Ld. of Bristow, my man standing by.[b]

Indorsed: Ld. Bristoll to L.-Coll. Mosely, 15 Janu: 1643.

(25.) THOMAS OGLE TO LIEUT.-COLONEL MOSELY.[c]

[Tanner MSS. vol. lxii. fol. 535. *Undated.*]

HONEST FREIND,

Last night I tarred at Court till past 11 a cloke. His Ma[tie] read, debated, consulted, upon the paper we booth signed; the result whereoff you have in this inclosed paper which I received from that Honourable Lord you write unto,[d] which yow must punctually observe, and in case my Lord Wharton should press yow to goe up

---

[a] 15 Jan. the date of this letter according to the indorsement, was Monday; the following Friday and Saturday would therefore be Jan. 19 and 20. On Sunday, the 21st, the royalist forces approached Aylesbury, and the allusion must relate to the design upon the town.

[b] These words are written in another hand to the letter.

[c] *See* Note to No. 23.

[d] His Majesty's instructions to Lieutenant-Colonel Mosely, to blow up the magazine, in case of sudden discovery, mentioned in the *Commons' Journals,* which may be identical with the document mentioned in the *Lords' Journals:* "The King's letter to Lieutenant-Colonel Mosely concerning the surrendering up to him of the town of Aylesbury."

about those coates yow must faine yourselfe sicke, and wholy intend the busines in hand. Send this bearer to me on Friday[a] without faile by whom Ile retourne the instrumentt, and for the dispatches you have for our frinds send them to London by your brother Sheifeild and pray send up ten pound to my wife that she may come to me; and write by your brother Sheifeild to my L. Essex ·secretary for a pass to be given your brother for Mrs. Marshall, her two children, and Mr. Welbye. I have here taken order for a wach one Mr. Simsone, which hath a pass to come to the French Ambassador[b] on Weddensday or Thursday. Pray therfore send away Mr. Sheifeild the morrow early and give our frinds all assurance of reallitie, but intimate nothinge of the busines in hand. I know your dexteritie and zeale attend the busines in hand   [Last words defaced.]

---

[a] Probably Friday, Jan. 19. The Royalist forces advanced towards Aylesbury on Sunday, Jan. 21. This letter is probably identical with "Captain Ogle's letter to Lieutenant-Colonel Mosely about the time of delivery up of the town," mentioned in the *Commons' Journals*, vol. iii. p. 378.

[b] The Prince of Harcourt, a special ambassador, came to England to mediate between the King and the Parliament. The two Houses, in answer to his overtures made through the Earl of Northampton, replied "that if the Prince D'Harcourt have anything to propose from the French King to the Lords and Commons assembled in the Parliament of England, the Houses have done nothing to bar or hinder the Prince D'Harcourt from the usual and fitting ways of address to them." Dec. 6· (C. J. vol. iii. pp. 319, 330.) As Charles at this time refused to recognise the two Houses as the Parliament of England, Harcourt's efforts to bring about a negociation were necessarily unavailing.

INDEX.